GUITAR ENSEMBLES

JAZZ CLASSICS

T0087235

Arrangements by Chip Henderson

ISBN 978-1-4584-1589-9

7777 W. BLUEMOUND RD. P.O. BOX 13819 MILWAUKEE, WI 53213

Visit Hal Leonard Online at
www.halleonard.com

CONTENTS

BAG'S NEW GROOVE

By Milt Jackson

CON ALMA

By John "Dizzy" Gillespie

THE DUKE

By Dave Brubeck

FOUR

By Miles Davis

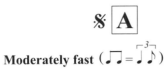

D.S. al Coda

Coda

C

GOODBYE PORK PIE HAT

By Charles Mingus

IN WALKED BUD

By Thelonious Monk

KILLER JOE
By Benny Golson

LITTLE SUNFLOWER

By Freddie Hubbard

MAIDEN VOYAGE
By Herbie Hancock

ON GREEN DOLPHIN STREET

Lyrics by Ned Washington
Music by Bronislau Kaper

SIDEWINDER

By Lee Morgan

STOLEN MOMENTS

Words and Music by Oliver Nelson

TAKE FIVE

By Paul Desmond

YARDBIRD SUITE

By Charlie Parker

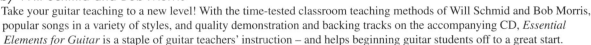

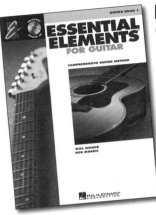

BOOK 1

Comprehensive Guitar Method
by Will Schmid and Bob Morris

Take your guitar teaching to a new level! With the time-tested classroom teaching methods of Will Schmid and Bob Morris, popular songs in a variety of styles, and quality demonstration and backing tracks on the accompanying CD, *Essential Elements for Guitar* is a staple of guitar teachers' instruction – and helps beginning guitar students off to a great start.

This method has been designed to meet the National Standards for Music Education, with features such as cross-curricular activities, quizzes, multicultural songs, basic improvisation and more. Concepts covered in Book 1 include: getting started; basic music theory; guitar chords; notes on each string; music history; ensemble playing; performance spotlights; and much more!

Songs used in Book 1 include such hits as: Dust in the Wind • Eleanor Rigby • Every Breath You Take • Hey Jude • Hound Dog • Let It Be • Ode to Joy • Rock Around the Clock • Stand by Me • Surfin' USA • Sweet Home Chicago • This Land Is Your Land • You Really Got Me • and more!

00862639 Book/CD Pack $17.99
00001173 Book Only $9.99

BOOK 2

Bob Morris

Essential Elements for Guitar, Book 2 is a continuation of the concepts and skills taught in Book 1 and includes all of its popular features as well – great songs in a variety of styles, a high-quality audio CD with demonstration and backing tracks, quizzes, music history, music theory, and much more. Concepts taught in Book 2 include: Playing melodically in positions up the neck; Playing movable chord shapes up the neck; Playing scales and extended chords in different keys; More right-hand studies – fingerpicking and pick style; Improvisation in positions up the neck; Studying different styles through great song selections; and more!

00865010 Book/CD Pack $17.99
00120873 Book Only $10.99

DAILY GUITAR WARM-UPS

by Tom Kolb
Mid-Beginner to Late Intermediate

This book contains a wide variety of exercises to help get your hands in top playing shape. It addresses the basic elements of guitar warm-ups by category: stretches and pre-playing coordination exercises, picking exercises, right and left-hand synchronization, and rhythm guitar warm-ups.

00865004 Book/CD Pack $9.99

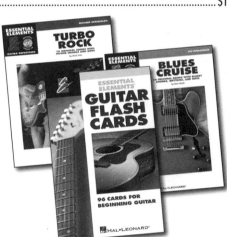

Essential Elements Guitar Ensembles

The songs in the Essential Elements Guitar Ensemble series are playable by three or more guitars. Each arrangement features the melody, a harmony part, and bass line in standard notation along with chord symbols. For groups with more than three or four guitars, the parts can be doubled. This series is perfect for classroom guitar ensembles or other group guitar settings.

J.S. BACH
00123103 Early Intermediate Level......................$9.99

THE BEATLES
00865008 Early Intermediate Level......................$9.99

BOSSA NOVA
00865006 Intermediate/Advanced Level...................$9.99

CHRISTMAS CLASSICS
00865015 Mid-Intermediate Level $9.99

CHRISTMAS SONGS
00001136 Mid-Beginner Level $9.95

CLASSICAL THEMES
00865005 Late Beginner Level..........................$9.99

DISNEY SONGS
00865014 Early Intermediate Level......................$9.99

EASY POP SONGS
00865011 Mid-Beginner Level $9.99

DUKE ELLINGTON
00865009 Mid-Intermediate Level $9.99

GREAT THEMES
00865012 Mid-Intermediate Level $9.99

JIMI HENDRIX
00865013 Mid-Intermediate Level $9.99

JAZZ BALLADS
00865002 Early Intermediate Level......................$9.99

JAZZ STANDARDS
00865007 Mid-Intermediate Level $9.99

POP HITS
00001128 Late Beginner Level.........................$9.99

ROCK CLASSICS
00865001 Late Beginner Level.........................$9.95

ROCK INSTRUMENTALS
00123102 Mid-Intermediate Level $9.99

TOP HITS
00130606 Early Intermediate Level......................$9.99

Flash Cards

96 CARDS FOR BEGINNING GUITAR
00865000...$7.95

Essential Elements Guitar Songs

The books in the Essential Elements Guitar Songs series feature popular songs specially selected for the practice of specific guitar chord types. Each book includes eight great songs and a CD with fantastic sounding play-along tracks. Practice at any tempo with the included Amazing Slow Downer software!

POWER CHORD ROCK
Mid-Beginner Level
00001139 Book/CD Pack $12.99

OPEN CHORD ROCK
Mid-Beginner Level
00001138 Book/CD Pack $12.99

BARRE CHORD ROCK
Late Beginner Level
00001137 Book/CD Pack $12.99

FOR MORE INFORMATION, SEE YOUR LOCAL MUSIC DEALER, OR WRITE TO:

HAL•LEONARD®
CORPORATION
7777 W. BLUEMOUND RD. P.O. BOX 13819 MILWAUKEE, WI 53213

Prices, contents, and availability subject to change without notice.

0315